# Cinderella Outgrows the Glass Slipper
## and Other
# Zany Fractured
# Fairy Tale Plays

### by J. M. Wolf

SCHOLASTIC
**PROFESSIONAL BOOKS**

NEW YORK • TORONTO • LONDON • AUCKLAND • SYDNEY
MEXICO CITY • NEW DELHI • HONG KONG • BUENOS AIRES

## ➣ DEDICATION ➣

Roses are Red,
Little Riding Hood is too.
I love you Mom,
and this one's for you!

## ➣ ACKNOWLEDGMENTS ➣

*Heartfelt thanks to Jeanie Davis Pullen for being my personal fairy godmother; Sarah Longhi at Scholastic, for her wonderful editorial skill and warm encouragement; Marsha Hatchett Burgeson for being our enthusiastic photographer; Kathleen Keating, for being my friend, cheerleader, and glue bottle; and most especially a big thank you to my wonderful class of fourth graders during the 2001–02 year. You put the magic in the pages that follow!*

Cover design by Maria Lilja
Cover and interior art by Mike Moran
Interior design by Solutions by Design, Inc.
Photography by Marsha Hatchett Burgeson

ISBN: 0-439-27168-1

7  8  9  10    40    08  07  06  05  04

# Table of Contents

# Introduction

## Why This Book?

"And they lived happily ever after..." has remained the enduring fairy-tale ending since fairy tales were first put into written form.

But in my own classroom when I'm teaching fairy tales, my favorite question is: "*Did* they live happily ever after?" And I invite you to ask the same question in the pages that follow. Here you will discover "happily ever after" not to be an ending, but a beginning point for creative writing and critical-thinking activities through readers' theater.

Fairy tales are a rich part of our literary history and have been my favorite stories since childhood. As a teacher, I have discovered fairy tales to be the perfect springboard for the study of the changing (and unchanging) values and ideologies of a society, as well as an ideal beginning point for creative writing and theater activities.

Theater has been a part of both my elementary and middle-school classrooms. I believe firmly in its value as a teaching tool. Over the years, I have watched shy and uneasy students blossom when given the chance to hone their speaking abilities. I have watched groups of loosely associated children become a cemented community through the common goal of reading scripts together. I have watched students who struggle with reading gain confidence as they practice and master simple readers' theater scripts. Theater, in and of itself, can be a magical experience for children. When combined with the magic inherent in fairy tales, an invaluable teaching opportunity is born.

## How Do I Use This Book?

You will notice immediately that the following readers' theater plays are not traditional fairy tales. Indeed, they have been written to help your students look at fairy tales from a different perspective, always with the question of "what if" in mind. What if, for example, Cinderella had never married the prince but had become a veterinarian instead? What if the Big Bad Wolf had become a teacher instead of pursuing a career as a "bad" wolf?

The scripts provide both engaging and flexible reading material that can be used with a whole class or in small groups. Included are specific parts easily managed by students with special needs. Use the levels indicated in the cast box on each teacher's page to help support the reading needs of your students.

You may wish to use the scripts in traditional readers' theater style, allowing kids to read informally from them. Or, you may wish to tackle a bigger theater project and create an elaborate evening production, complete with sets, costumes, and invitations, for families to attend. I've included easy ideas to help you create such a production in the Resources! section on page 67. The choice is yours.

An added treasure following each play are creative writing ideas that align with the NCTE language arts/English standards. Particularly, you will notice writing activities that address Standards 2, 4, and 5: reading a wide range of literature from different periods and genres, communicating with different audiences through speech, and writing for different audiences for a variety of purposes.

*Presenting the plays and engaging in the writing activities in this book help your students meet Language Arts Standards 2, 4, and 5.*

Please also note the bibliography at the end of the book, which highlights just a few of the wonderful children's traditional and nontraditional fairy tale books available as well as some interesting adult fairy tale theory books you may enjoy perusing.

Within this book, I hope you and your students discover the magic and fun inherent in both fairy tales and theater. It is an exciting discovery worth pursuing, one that begins where traditional fairy tales end.

Happily,
J.M. Wolf

*Cast of "Once Upon a Hundred-Year's Nap"*

*Cast of "Two Pigs, a Wolf, and a Mud Pie"*

*Cast of "Reading, Writing,...and Little Red Riding Hood"*

# Cinderella Outgrows the Glass Slipper

## Getting Started!

## Introduction

In this play, Cinderella dreams not about going to a ball, but about going to school to become a veterinarian. This play twists the traditional Cinderella story, so that your students will find Cinderella's real work comes from convincing her fairy godmothers that she knows what is best for herself.

### Costume Ideas

**Cinderella:** ragged clothing with a broom, dust mop, or bucket; fancier clothing with athletic shoes for scene 3.

**Stepsisters:** fancier clothes than Cinderella, exaggerated make-up, eye masks, or colored face cream for scene 2. In this scene, actors may also carry teddy bears and pretend to suck their thumbs.

**Fairy Godmothers:** magic wands, wings made from nylon-covered hangers. Wings can become bent throughout the play to show how hard the fairies are working.

### Set Ideas

**Cinderella's kitchen**, may have a table and chairs, along with a clock, "stove," or other kitchen items. Narrators in all scenes sit or stand, one on either side of the stage, so that the audience can see them and the action of the play. When the stepsisters are sleeping, they may lie on blankets on the floor or on beds fashioned out of chairs, tables, or desks. They may have pillows, teddy bears, slippers, clothes and toys strewn about, or other things found in a bedroom. During the ball scene, there may be an *hors d'oeuvres* table, with paper food. The school band or orchestra may provide a small ensemble to pantomime playing instruments during the ball.

---

## THE CAST

- ⚱ Narrator #1
- ⚱ Narrator #2
- ⚱ Cinderella
- ⚱ Fairy Godmother #1
- ⚱ Fairy Godmother #2
- ⚱⚱ Fairy Godmother #3
- ⚱⚱ Butternut (stepsister)
- ⚱⚱ Hazelnut (stepsister)
- ⚱⚱ Prince
- ⚱⚱⚱ Oscar
- ⚱⚱⚱ Butler
- ⚱⚱⚱ Jeeves
- ⚱⚱⚱ Sign Walkers (4)
- ⚱⚱⚱ Partygoers (3 or more)
- ⚱⚱⚱ Sound Effects

---

⚱ *Role with challenging speaking part*

⚱⚱ *Role with fewer lines*

⚱⚱⚱ *Nonspeaking part or part with few words which may be appropriate for students with limited English proficiency or with special needs.*

# Cinderella Outgrows the Glass Slipper

## The Script!

## The Cast

| | |
|---|---|
| Sign Walker # 1 | Fairy Godmother #2 |
| Narrator #1 | Oscar |
| Narrator #2 | Jeeves |
| Cinderella | Sign Walker #3 |
| Fairy Godmother #1 | Butler |
| Sign Walker #2 | Prince |
| Hazelnut | Sign Walker #4 |
| Butternut | Fairy Godmother #3 |

## ☙ SCENE ONE ❧

# Cinderella's Kitchen

**Sign Walker #1:** Student walks across stage with the sign "Scene 1: Cinderella's Kitchen."

*(Narrators enter and take positions. Cinderella enters and begins sweeping.)*

**Narrator #1:** (*to audience*) Once upon a time, there was a young woman named Cinderella, who lived with her stepmother and two stepsisters, Butternut and Hazelnut. Both stepsisters and their mother treated Cinderella as if she were their maid. Every day they forced her to scrub and polish and clean and do whatever else they wanted her to do.

**Narrator #2:** (*to audience*) Despite this awful treatment, Cinderella worked cheerfully, because in her heart she had a secret wish. (*Cinderella stops sweeping and pretends to pet a cat in her arms.*) More than anything in the world, Cinderella wanted to become a veterinarian. Ever since she was a young child she had enjoyed taking care of animals.

**Narrator #1:** So after she finished her chores each night, she would stay up late and mend the neighbor's shoes for money. She saved each penny so she could someday afford to follow her dream. Little did she know, however, that soon things were about to change forever.

**Narrator #2:** Because one day, as Cinderella was sweeping and dreaming about her career, suddenly…(*Enter Fairy Godmother #1.*)

**Cinderella:** Who are you??

**Fairy Godmother #1:** Why child, I am your fairy godmother. I am here to grant your greatest wish!

**Narrator #1:** At last! Cinderella thought this was her chance to become a veterinarian.

**Cinderella:** Great! What I'd really like to do is become a…

**Fairy Godmother #1:** (*interrupting*) Oh I know, I know. Don't worry about a thing. I've taken care of everything! You are going to the ball tomorrow night where you will meet a handsome prince, fall madly in love, get married, have half a dozen kids (*Cinderella makes a face*), and live happily ever after.

**Cinderella:** No, but, but…I want…

**Fairy Godmother #1:** (*interrupting*) There's no need to thank me, dear. I'm just doing my job. I've got to be off now. There's a prince who's having a hard time waking up a beauty. I'll take care of everything and check in on you later.

**Narrator #2:** And so the fairy godmother left Cinderella to sweep and clean and think about many things.

(*Cinderella exits, sweeping and thinking.*)

## ☞ SCENE TWO ☜

# Stepsisters' Bedroom

(*Stepsisters enter and pretend to sleep.*)

**Sign Walker # 2:** Student walks across stage with the sign "Scene 2: Stepsisters' Bedrooms: The Next Day."

**Narrator #2:** After spending the night in deep thought, Cinderella came up with a great way to get out of going to the ball so she could continue her own dream. First, she went to the room where her oldest stepsister, Hazelnut, was sleeping.

**Cinderella:** (*shaking Hazelnut*) Hazelnut, it's time to wake up!

**Hazelnut:** Huh? Oh you! Go away!

**Cinderella:** Say, Hazelnut, I was thinking. How would you like a great fairy godmother to help you catch that handsome prince at the ball tonight?

**Hazelnut:** Me? You think *I* need a fairy godmother? Why, the prince will take one look at this beautiful face and fall instantly in love. I don't need any help. Now go get my oat bran for breakfast! (*She goes back to sleep.*)

**Narrator #1:** But Cinderella wasn't about to give up that easily! Next, she tried her other stepsister, Butternut.

**Cinderella:** (*cheerfully*) Butternut! Time to wake up! (*Butternut wakes up.*) Say, Butternut, I was thinking. Wouldn't a fairy godmother be just the thing for the ball tonight? Hmm?

**Butternut:** Now why would I need a fairy godmother? Everyone knows I am the most beautiful woman in the kingdom. Silly girl. You've been spending too much time in the cinders again. Now run along and make my oatmeal!

**Cinderella:** (*snaps her fingers*) Darn!!!

(*Fairy Godmother #2 enters.*)

**Fairy Godmother #2:** Hello dear! How are you?

**Cinderella:** (*to audience*) Now what?! (*to Fairy Godmother #2*) Who are you?

**Fairy Godmother #2:** Oh, your fairy godmother sent me. Poor dear. Has a dreadful cold. I'm one of the substitute fairies on duty tonight. But don't worry. She told me what you want. I'm on a tight schedule now, dear, so hurry hurry. It's off you go to start getting ready for the ball. I already have your footmen ready. (*yelling*) Oscar! Jeeves!

(*Enter Oscar and Jeeves, crawling on all fours.*)

**Fairy Godmother #2:** (*to Oscar and Jeeves*) Get up, get up. I keep telling you you're not dogs anymore! You're footmen for the coach tonight!

**Oscar:** (*stands*) Woof.

**Jeeves:** (*stands*) Woof. Woof.

**Cinderella:** (*to Fairy Godmother #2*) Are you *sure* you're up to this?

**Fairy Godmother #2:** (*pulling Cinderella off-stage*) Come on!

## ᔆ SCENE THREE ᔆ

# The Ball

(*Partygoers enter and act as if they are at a party. Prince enters with stepsisters on either side of him.*)

**Sign Walker #3:** Student walks across stage with the sign "Scene 3: The Ball, That Night."

**Narrator #2:** And so came the big day of the ball. All the women from the kingdom arrived wearing their finest clothes to impress the prince. The substitute fairy godmother had created a beautiful new outfit for Cinderella, along with a stunning pair of glass slippers.

**Narrator #1:** But Cinderella refused to wear the slippers, choosing instead a pair she made herself using leather scraps saved from her customers. If she had to go to the ball, she decided, she would at least wear comfortable shoes.

**Fairy Godmother #2:** (*nudging and pushing Cinderella on stage*) Good-bye, dear. Have a good time now. I'll see you at midnight!

**Cinderella:** But I don't want to…(*stops to see that people are staring*). Oh…Hello!

**Butler:** (*to Cinderella*) Announcing Ms.—?

**Cinderella:** (*to the butler*) Ah… (*stops and thinks*) Ms…er-a-ble?

**Butler:** Ms. Erable! (*Party goers clap briefly.*)

**Hazelnut:** (*pointing at Cinderella*) Hey! That girl looks awfully familiar.

**Butternut:** You know, you're right!

**Prince:** (*points to Cinderella*) Beautiful!

**Hazelnut and Butternut:** (*to prince*) What?!

**Prince:** (*to Cinderella*) Incredible!

**Hazelnut and Butternut:** Wha—?! (*exit off-stage, crying*)

**Prince:** (*to Cinderella*) Ms. Erable, I must say…

(*Clock begins to sound. Clock sounds only to ten.*)

**Cinderella:** Oh, gosh, midnight already? Gotta run! (*exits off-stage, losing a shoe in the process*)

**Prince:** No, wait! It's only ten o'clock. I must know… (*Prince runs off-stage, chasing Cinderella.*)

**Narrator #2:** But it was too late. Cinderella was already well on her way home, assisted by her two trusty footmen, Oscar and Jeeves. (*Barks are heard from off-stage.*)

## ⌒ SCENE FOUR ⌒

# Cinderella's Kitchen

**Sign Walker #4:** Student walks across stage with the sign, "Scene 4: Cinderella's Kitchen, Two Weeks Later."

(*Enter Cinderella, cleaning.*)

**Narrator #1:** Several weeks passed after the ball, and Cinderella's life was back to normal. She often thought of her narrow miss with the prince and was glad to be back working at her dream of becoming a vet.

**Narrator #2:** Then one day, as Cinderella was in her kitchen sweeping, who should appear but . . .

(*Enter Fairy Godmother #3, cautiously.*)

**Cinderella:** (*to fairy godmother*) Oh, great. Don't tell me. You're a fairy godmother.

**Fairy Godmother #3:** Well, yes. I've been sent by the head office. The other two fairies refused to come back.

**Cinderella:** Look, lady. I never wanted to go to the ball. I don't like dressing up. I never asked your agency to get involved in my life. And I'm too young to get married to a perfect stranger, even if he is a prince!

**Fairy Godmother #3:** Well! What kind of princess are you, anyway? You're lucky I don't turn you into a toad right here. I can see why no one at the agency wants to work here. I quit! (*begins to exit, bumps into Prince, who enters.*)

**Fairy Godmother #3:** (*to prince*) Don't bother with her, dear. She's a lost cause. Can I interest you in a poison apple?

**Prince:** (*to Fairy Godmother #3*) Ah, no thanks! (*to Cinderella*) At last! I have found you!

**Cinderella:** (*to audience*) Can this day get any worse?

**Prince:** You didn't let me finish what I was saying at the ball. I've been searching for you for weeks! (*taking out shoe, lowering to one knee*) I've never seen a more beautiful pair of comfortable shoes.

**Cinderella:** Huh?

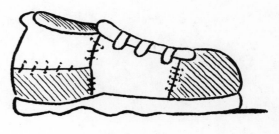

**Prince:** Your shoes! They look so comfortable! You don't know how long I have searched for a decent pair of shoes. You wouldn't believe the horrible shoes the royal shoesmith makes! All those diamonds and stuff. Yuck! I hear you are quite the shoe maker. I must have a pair. Please. I'll pay anything!

**Cinderella:** Now that's the first sensible thing I've heard from anyone in a long time. Get up. Get up! (*leads prince off-stage*) Let me show you my shoe shop.

**Narrator #1:** A week later, Cinderella delivered a brand new pair of shoes to the prince. After seeing them, the king and queen decided they wanted a pair, too, and within a month, Cinderella had enough money to leave home and go to vet school where she passed with flying colors. As for her fairy godmothers...

**Narrator #2:** Her first fairy godmother never returned to the agency. Instead, she joined the local tooth-fairy union and has been happily collecting teeth ever since.

**Narrator #1:** The second fairy godmother was called upon by Hazelnut and Butternut to find them princes. It turned out to be a two-fairy job, and the third fairy godmother was called in from retirement to help. Both girls eventually found husbands who cooked and cleaned for them while they sat around looking through magazines. And, as they say...

**Narrator #2:** Everyone lived happily ever after.

# Language Arts Activity Page

### ⚜ ACTIVITY ONE ⚜

## The Party Was a Ball!

**DESCRIPTIVE WRITING: Building a paragraph with details**

Even though Cinderella didn't want to go to the ball, many people love parties. Let students use the ball scene as a springboard to collect ideas to write their own descriptive paragraphs about their ultimate party.

In their planning, encourage students to use their imaginations. Explain that things such as cost, location, and transportation will not be barriers in their planning. Their party can take place in a tropical rainforest or underwater in a submarine if they wish.

Begin by brainstorming one or two things at the party that will fall into each of the five senses categories. For example, for the sense of sound, students might hear music if they are at a house, or the sounds of a rainforest if their party is in a faraway place. For the sense of touch, they might feel the coolness of water if they are swimming, or the heaviness of a ball if they are bowling.

Next, distribute The Perfect Party Planner reproducible (page 17) and let students organize their ideas on paper. They should include details from all five senses, as well as their feelings about the party, in their paragraphs. As they organize their ideas into a paragraph, remind them that the object is to create writing that is detailed enough so readers will experience the party as if they were there.

( Extend it! ) Students may contrast a party they would plan in the present with a party they would plan if they had lived in the past. What would the ultimate party have looked like if students had lived as pilgrims? Or during King Arthur's time? How would they plan a party without electricity, modern transportation, or plumbing?

### ⚜ ACTIVITY TWO ⚜

## To Whom It May Concern

**PERSUASIVE WRITING: Writing to Persuade a Specific Audience**

It was obvious the fairy godmothers misunderstood Cinderella in this play. Give students the opportunity to help the fairy godmothers understand Cinderella by having them write a persuasive letter to the fairy godmothers explaining why she should not have to attend the ball.

Ask students to think of up to three arguments to present to the fairy godmothers about why Cinderella should be allowed to pursue her own dreams. For example, students might suggest that she will be financially independent as a vet, or that she is too young to get married, or that she has never met the prince.

Next, ask students to generate supporting details for each argument and then form these details into letters written to the fairy godmothers.

**Extend it!** Students may wish to write a persuasive letter to a different character from the play. For example, they may wish to write to Cinderella, explaining to her why she should attend the ball. Or they may try writing a letter to the prince, explaining why he should consider dating one of the stepsisters.

## ❧ ACTIVITY THREE ❧

# Did They Live Happily Ever After?

### NARRATIVE WRITING: Developing Plot

What happens to Cinderella after the play ends? Will she fulfill her dream and become a veterinarian? Will her fairy godmothers be happy in their new jobs? Give your students the chance to answer these questions for themselves by writing their own "happily ever after" story.

There are many delightful picture books that show how authors play with the structure of an established story and use the conclusion of a traditional fairy tale as the introduction for a new problem. Jon Scieszka does this in *The Frog Prince Continued* (Scholastic, 1991), as does Diane Stanley in *Rumpelstiltskin's Daughter* (William Morrow, 1997). *Cinder Edna* by Ellen Jackson (William Morrow, 1994) creates a new twist on the whole Cinderella story, adding a new problem at the conclusion of the traditional tale.

Jon Scieszka does this in *The Frog Prince Continued*, as does Diane Stanley in *Rumpelstiltskin's Daughter*. *Cinder Edna*, by Ellen Jackson, creates a new twist on the whole Cinderella story, adding a new problem at the conclusion of the traditional tale.

After sharing one or more of these books with students, ask them to brainstorm things they imagine might happen after the play ends. Remind students to focus on the plot and introduce a new problem into the story. For example, perhaps the stepsisters get divorced and move in with Cinderella, or Cinderella discovers she doesn't like being a vet and searches for a new career path. Keep students focused on developing plot with a solid beginning, middle, and end. Use the What Happens After "Happily Ever After"? organizer (page 66) to help students plan their stories.

**Extend it!** As an extension, students may wish to finish a different traditional fairy tale of their choice, developing a new problem that begins at the conclusion of the fairy tale. Stories may be read aloud to the class or put into a class collection of play continuations.

Name_____  Date _____

# The Perfect Party Planner!

We're told that Cinderella managed to make it to the party of her life. …Ever thought of planning a party like that? What if you could plan the ultimate party—anywhere you like, with unlimited funds, and invite anyone you choose, including fairy-tale characters! Fill out the invitation to get your ideas flowing (try to make your party unique by thinking of an unusual—even imaginary!—location and an unusual event or theme). Then, in the 5-senses chart below, brainstorm all the details you can think of that someone attending your party would experience.

## You're Invited to a Party!

The Event: _____
(title of your party)

The Time: _____

The Place: _____

Who's coming: _____

Special Attire: _____
(If guests will need to dress up or bring special equipment or gear, let them know!)

Hosted by _____
(Your name)

## Describe Your Party! 5-Senses

 I'd see…

 I'd hear…

I'd smell…

 I'd taste…

 I'd feel…

# Two Pigs, a Wolf, and a Mud Pie

## Getting Started!

### Introduction

**In this play, one of the three little pigs is missing and the Big Bad Wolf is the suspect. Your students will enjoy the twists and turns this story takes as the two remaining pigs step in and out of fairy tales to search for their missing sibling and all three pigs discover that things are not always as they seem.**

**Costume Ideas**

**Tic, Tac, and Toe (the pigs):** pink "animal" attire (i.e., ears made out of construction paper, pipe cleaner tails, matching shirts—stained, if possible!). When searching for their missing sibling, pigs may carry a magnifying glass, notebook, trench coat, camera, or other "detective" items.

**Wolf:** brown "animal" attire. For more animal costume ideas, see Resources! on page 67.

**Set Ideas** There are a number of places where living props may be used to include more students in nonspeaking parts. In Scene 2, students can become forest trees or gingerbread cookies by posing as such or holding cardboard cutouts of trees or cookies. A student may cameo as the witch selling apples to Snow White and walk past the pigs as they make their way to Snow White's cottage. In Scene 3, students may hold business signs to form the town "street" that the pigs walk down. They may advertise fairy tale businesses such as "Jack's Climbing Service" or "Alice in Wonderland's Mirror Shop."

**Narrators** sit or stand throughout the play, one on either side of the stage, so that the audience can see them and the action of the play.

In the forest scene, two "houses" are needed, one for Hansel and Gretel, and one for Snow White. For ideas, see Resources! page 67.

During the dance scene, you may wish to have chairs, decorations, a banquet table, and an outline of a grandfather clock. Extra students may stand in as partygoers.

**THE CAST**

- 8 Wolf (narrator)
- 8 Tic (narrator)
- 8 Tac
- 8 Toe
- 88 Snow White
- 88 Cinderella
- 88 Witch
- 88 Hansel
- 88 Gretel
- 888 Prince
- 888 Sign Walker #1
- 888 Sign Walker #2
- 888 Sign Walker #3
- 888 Sign Walker #4
- 888 Sound Technicians (door knock, clock tone)

*8 Role with challenging speaking part*

*88 Role with fewer lines*

*888 Nonspeaking part or part with few words which may be appropriate for students with limited English proficiency or with special needs.*

*Note: Wolf and three pigs can be played as male or female parts. Modify script accordingly.*

# Two Pigs, a Wolf, and a Mud Pie

## The Script!

### The Cast

| | |
|---|---|
| Sign Walker #1 | Hansel |
| Wolf (narrator) | Witch |
| Tic (narrator) | Snow White |
| Tac | Sign Walker #3 |
| Toe | Cinderella |
| Sign Walker #2 | Prince |
| Gretel | Sign Walker #4 |

# The House of the Three Little Pigs

*(Wolf and Tic enter and each sit on their designated narrating spots.)*

**Sign Walker #1:** Student walks across stage with the sign, "Scene 1: The House of the Three Little Pigs."

**Wolf:** (*to audience*) Hi! My name is Ima. Ima Wolf. And we have a story to tell you about three little pigs.

**Tic:** (*to audience*) Actually, it's a story about two little pigs.

**Wolf:** Yes, right. As I was saying: We have a story to tell you about two little pigs.

**Tic:** You see, my name is Tic, and I live with my two brothers, Tac and Toe. And one day, not so long ago, we were just three little pigs living quite happily in my brick house, until my brothers decided to go grocery shopping.

**Wolf:** Being pigs, they were craving mud pies and had heard there was a big sale on dark rich mud at the grocery store. Tac and Toe left the house to get groceries, while Tic stayed behind to get the kitchen ready.

**Tic:** And when my brothers got back to our house, they made a discovery that starts our story.

*(Tac and Toe enter together.)*

**Tac:** Whew! Can you believe the checkout line at the Grab and Pay? I thought we were never going to get out of there!

**Toe:** No kidding! And did you see that sale on pork chops? Yuck! Let's get these to Tic so he can start baking.

**Tac:** (*yelling*) Tic! We've got the mud!!!

**Toe:** (*yelling*) Hey, Tic! We brought you some of your favorite ice cream, Stupendous Pig-sty, with Extra Dirt Clumps!

(*Tac and Toe look around house.*)

**Tic:** (*to audience*): You see, what they didn't know was that I wasn't home then.

**Wolf:** (to audience) He was with me.

**Tac:** (*to Toe*) He's not here!

**Toe:** (*to Tac*) Oh no!...Do you think?

**Tac and Toe:** (together) The big bad wolf has him!

(*Tac and Toe search the house and exit.*)

**Tic:** Well, my two brothers hurried off to find me, worried that I had been kidnapped by the wolf.

**Wolf:** And that's when the real fun began!

(*Tac and Toe continue looking as they exit.*)

## ◠ SCENE TWO ◠

# The Enchanted Forest

**Sign Walker #2:** Student walks across stage with the sign, "Scene 2: The Enchanted Forest."

(*Tac and Toe enter, searching for Tic.*)

**Tic:** My brothers searched and searched for me, until they came to the Enchanted Forest.

**Wolf:** A place that even wolves don't like to visit.

**Tic:** But, desperate to find me, they went in anyway. For hours they looked, and just about the time they thought they were too tired to go on, they found a house. (Tac and Toe stop at gingerbread house.)

**Tac:** (*to Toe, sniffing*) Hey, do I smell...

**Toe:** Gingerbread! Yum! (Both pigs pretend to eat the house.) I love the chocolatey trim around the windows!

*(Hansel and Gretel enter.)*

**Gretel:** Hey! What do you think you're doing? (Tac and Toe stop eating.)

**Hansel:** Yeah, this is the part where we eat the house.

**Tac:** You wouldn't happen to be Hansel would you? (Hansel nods yes)

**Toe:** Are you Gretel? (she nods)

**Tac:** Have either of you seen a pig, about so high?

**Toe:** We think he may have been taken by a big bad wolf to be made into dinner.

**Hansel and Gretel:** (together) No.

*(Witch enters or appears at house door.)*

**Witch:** Hansel, Gretel! Come in, dears. I have been expecting you!

**Tac:** Wait! Stop!

**Toe:** I've read this book! Don't go in there! She's really a wi— *(Hansel and Gretel follow the witch.)*

**Witch:** *(exits with Hansel and Gretel or leads them into the house)* I was just about to serve some ham dinners. (*Tac and Toe walk away quickly.*)

**Tic:** Well, you can bet my brothers got out of there in a hurry!

**Wolf:** They kept walking until they came to a second house.

**Tic:** At this house, they noticed seven tiny pairs of socks hanging on a clothesline outside.

**Wolf:** Inside, they could hear someone singing. (*Snow White whistles or hums.*)

**Tac:** This house looks safe.

**Toe:** It sounds friendly. (*sniffs*) And I don't smell any gingerbread.

(*Toe knocks on the door.*)

**Snow White:** (*from door*) Yes? May I help you?

**Toe:** Hello, Ma'am. We're here today…

**Snow White:** (*interrupts*) I don't want any!

**Tac:** (*through the door*) Ma'am were just looking for…

**Snow White:** Are you selling apples? Because some nasty old lady just tried to get me to eat one of her apples, and before that, some guy showed up wanting me to try to guess his name, and I haven't gotten one thing done today!

**Toe:** We're not selling apples. We're looking for our brother.

**Tac:** We think he may have been taken by a wolf.

**Toe:** And we're terribly worried about what is going to happen to him. Have you seen him?

**Snow White:** Oh, how awful. I'm so sorry to hear that! What does your brother look like?

**Tac:** He's a pig.

**Snow White:** That's not very nice.

**Toe:** No really, he's a pig.

**Snow White:** Oh. Well I haven't seen anyone all day except for very pesky sales people. I'm sorry that I can't be of more help, but I really do have to get back to my work. Good luck!

**Tic:** And so, once again, my brothers continued walking through the forest, getting more and more worried.

(*Pigs continue to walk across stage, searching, and then exit.*)

## ◠ SCENE THREE ◠
# Cinderella's Town

**Sign Walker #3:** Student walks across stage with the sign, "Scene 3: Cinderella's Town."

**Wolf:** Well, the two brothers searched the entire forest without any luck until, at last, just as it was getting dark, they left the forest and found themselves in a small town.

**Tic:** They noticed that no one was around. All the houses looked empty, and the only light at all was coming from a castle on the edge of town.

**Wolf:** Carefully, the pigs made their way to the castle…

**Tic:** …where they walked right in to the middle of a festive ball.

(*Tac and Toe enter the party.*)

**Toe:** Look at the food!

**Tac:** Not now! We have to find Tic! (*Tac approaches a party member.*) Excuse me, have you seen… (*The clock interrupts, striking midnight. Cinderella runs past and drops a shoe.*)

**Toe:** (*to Cinderella*) Hey, you dropped this!

**Cinderella:** (*grabs shoe and throws it back on the floor*) No, no! It's supposed to stay there. You're going to ruin the story! (*Cinderella exits.*)

**Prince:** (*running after Cinderella with shoe*) Wait! Don't leave!

**Tac:** (*to prince*) Have you seen our brother?

**Toe:** He's been taken by a big bad wolf!

**Prince:** A wolf?! Oh my! I must find that girl and protect her! (*in the direction of Cinderella*) Wait! Wait! You lost your shoe!...and there's a wolf out there! (*He exits.*)

**Tac:** (*to Toe*) Now what?

**Wolf:** The two pigs felt hopeless.

**Tic:** They had gone as far as they could and knew it was time to go back home.

(*Tac and Toe exit sadly.*)

### ⌒ SCENE FOUR ⌒

# The Three Little Pigs' House

**Sign Walker #4:** Student walks across stage with the sign, "Scene 4: The House of the Three Little Pigs."

**Wolf:** By the time Tac and Toe got home, it was the next morning.

**Tic:** And when they walked into that little brick house, feeling sad and tired and lonely, they were in for a huge surprise.

**Wolf:** Because Tic and I were waiting for them in the kitchen.

(*Wolf and Tic enter set. Tac and Toe enter.*)

**Toe:** Tic!

**Tac:** It's the wolf! Get away from Tic, you howling bag of bones!

**Tic:** (*to Tac and Toe*) What are you two doing? Where have you been? I've been worried sick about you! Didn't you read my note?

**Tac and Toe:** (*look at each other*) Note? (look at Wolf) Note?

**Wolf:** Yes, the note. The one that says Tic is helping me fix my flat tire and directions for where we are so you can find us and not to worry.

**Tac and Toe:** Oh.

**Tic:** Ima's car broke down outside our house right after you left and I took him to the station to get a new tire. You didn't think he...

**Wolf:** You didn't think I ate Tic, did you?

**Tac and Toe:** Well...

**Tic:** Oh, no, this guy is a vegetarian! While we were waiting for you, he showed me how to make the best spinach pie.

**Wolf:** Here, try some.

**Tac:** (*sniffs, then takes a bite*) Gee, thanks!

**Tic:** (*to audience*) So there you have it, the story of the two little pigs.

**Wolf:** (*to audience*) And of course, you know how it ends.

**Toe:** (*to audience*) Everyone lives...

**Tac:** (*to audience*)...happily ever after.

# Language Arts Activity Page

## Curtain Call!

### ❧ ACTIVITY ONE ❧

## Finding Your Way Through the Forest

### DESCRIPTIVE WRITING: Using Adjectives and Adverbs

A lack of communication proved to be quite a problem in the lives of the three little pigs in this play. Give your students the chance to practice writing clear and concise descriptions of various locations from the play so they will not have similar problems.

Begin by brainstorming locations that would lend themselves to detailed descriptions, such as the pigs' house, the forest, the witch's house, Snow White's house, Cinderella's hometown, the ballroom, or the prince's castle.

Using a 5-senses chart like the one on page 17, ask students to pick a location and fill in the chart using all five of their senses. For example, what does the house of the little pigs smell like? What is the temperature? Is it extremely neat or pig-like? What kind of music might be playing? Ask students to fill in at least two things for each sense and write a detailed description of their chosen locations using adjectives for each of the senses. Remind students that the goal is to help readers of the paragraph experience the location as if they were there.

### ❧ ACTIVITY TWO ❧

## Dear Sirs,

### EXPOSITORY: Writing to Explain

In this play, the two pig brothers discovered the importance of being able to write (and read) notes. Give students the opportunity to practice developing their own skills in informative letter writing by asking them to write a fairy-tale letter that leaves instructions or gives directions.

Begin by brainstorming a list of dangerous or scary situations from the play, such as staying away from the enchanted forest and witches, or checking to make sure there is a spare tire in the car. Using the Friendly Fairy-Tale Letter format on page 29 as a guide, instruct students to write a letter to one of the characters from the play detailing how to avoid or remedy the situation in which they find themselves. You may wish to make this assignment a formal letter writing activity and require that letters include a proper heading, date, and indented body.

**Extend it!** Using the same format, students may write about situations found in other fairy tales, such as how to get seven people ready for work in the morning ("Snow White"); proper "ball" behavior and etiquette ("Cinderella"); how to select the best mud pie from the grocery store ("The Three Little Pigs"); or warning signs to look for that might indicate there is a witch inside a house ("Hansel and Gretel").

After the letters are written, you may wish to pair students and let them write responses to each other's letters.

## ❧ ACTIVITY THREE ❧
# Mud Pies vs. Apple Pies

### PERSUASIVE WRITING: Expressing Personal Opinion in Writing

Was it a good idea for the two pigs to go dashing off through a dangerous forest on their own? Some readers might argue that the risk was worth it, while others would contend that it was foolish. In this activity, give students the opportunity to decide for themselves and write persuasively about fairy-tale situations.

Begin by creating a class list of "controversial" situations from the play. For example, was it wrong for a hungry pig to eat a gingerbread house? Should Snow White have taken time out of her busy schedule to help the pigs? Are wolves such innately dangerous creatures that one should always avoid them?

You also may wish to brainstorm ideas from other fairy tales. For example, was it wrong for Jack to climb the beanstalk and steal from the giant? Was it okay for Rumpelstiltskin to demand the queen's baby as payment for his favor?

After you have a list, let students pick one to write about. Encourage them to use their imaginations and create at least two solid reasons for why they chose their positions. Students should write at least one paragraph in support of their viewpoints.

**Extend it!** To stretch thinking (and perspective) skills, ask students to write about both sides of one issue, creating at least two solid arguments for each side.

When complete, students' writing may be used as a springboard for a class debate or panel discussion about one of these issues.

# Friendly Fairy-Tale Letter

So, you don't like the way the first two pigs built their houses? Or the way Snow White took an apple from a stranger? It's your turn to give your favorite fairy-tale character a piece of your mind in a friendly letter!

Pick a character and something this character did that caused a problem. In the space below, write a letter to this character explaining the problem and recommending what he or she might do to avoid this problem in the future.

_____

_____
date

Dear _____,
fairy-tale character

_____

_____

_____

_____

_____

_____

_____

_____

Sincerely,

_____
your name

# Reading, Writing,...and Little Red Riding Hood

### Getting Started!

## Introduction

The Big Bad Wolf gets his chance to shine in new ways in this play as he interacts with Little Red Riding Hood and discovers a new career: kindergarten teacher.

### Costume Ideas

**Little Red Riding Hood:** red scarf, hood, necklace, or hat. She can carry a basket with a pretend or real cell phone. She can carry a red handkerchief or napkin to leave with the wolf at the end of the play.

**Young Wolf:** grey or brown "animal" attire. For more animal costume ideas, see Resources! on page 67.

**Wolf:** teacher garb (button-down shirt or blouse and matching pants or skirt) over "animal" attire.

**Inspector Frank:** large overcoat with hat or badge, glasses, and magnifying glass.

**Woodcutter:** "knickers" (pants that stop at the knee or are rolled up), a plaid shirt, and a stocking cap (Paul Bunyan style). He can carry an ax (made of cardboard or construction paper) or a piece of chopped wood.

**Goldilocks:** yellow curls made out of yarn or a blonde wig.

### THE CAST

- ⚬ Young Wolf
- ⚬ Little Red
- ⚬ Older Wolf
- ⚬⚬ Inspector Frank
- ⚬⚬ Goldilocks
- ⚬⚬ Woodcutter
- ⚬⚬⚬ Kids 1, 2, and 3
- ⚬⚬⚬ Sign Walker #1
- ⚬⚬⚬ Sign Walker #2
- ⚬⚬⚬ Sign Walker #3
- ⚬⚬⚬ Sign Walker #4
- ⚬⚬⚬ Kids
- ⚬⚬⚬ Sound Technicians (door knocks, cell phone tone)

---

⚬ *Role with challenging speaking part*

⚬⚬ *Role with fewer lines*

⚬⚬⚬ *Nonspeaking part or part with few words which may be appropriate for students with limited English proficiency or with special needs.*

**Note:** Wolf can be played by a male or female; modify script accordingly.

### Set Ideas
Students may pose as **living props** to create the forest of trees outside the grandmother's house. In the classroom scenes at the opening and ending of the play, the wolf may sit on a teacher's chair. Other props may include student desks, a blackboard (on wheels), a flag, or other things typically found in a classroom. At grandmother's house, you can create an elaborate house or an imaginary one (for ideas, see Resources! on page 67).

# Reading, Writing,...and Little Red Riding Hood

## The Script!

## The Cast

| | | |
|---|---|---|
| Kid 1 | Sign Walker #2 | Inspector Frank |
| Wolf | Young Wolf | Sign Walker #3 |
| Kid 2 | Little Red | Sign Walker #4 |
| Kid 3 | Woodcutter | |
| Sign Walker #1 | Goldilocks | |

## ⌒ SCENE ONE ⌒

# Mr. Wolf's Classroom

(*Three students gather around Mr. Wolf, who sits in a chair.*)

**Kid 1:** Tell us a story, Mr. Wolf!

**Wolf:** Do you want to hear a story, kindergartners?

**Kid 2:** Yes! Tell us a story.

**Wolf:** Well, okay, I'll tell you the story about how I became a kindergarten teacher.

**Kid 3:** You mean you weren't always a teacher?

**Wolf:** Oh, goodness no! My first job was with an agency that trained big bad wolves.

**Kid 1:** Really?

**Kid 2:** But you're not big and bad.

**Older Wolf:** That's all because of a little girl named Little Red Riding Hood.

**Kid 3:** Little Red Riding Hood?

**Wolf:** Yes. It happened about thirty years ago when I was sent on my very first job with the agency. Little Red Riding Hood had just arrived at her grandmother's house with a basket full of goodies. I was hiding in her grandmother's bed, waiting for the little girl to show up and....

(*Actors freeze.*)

## ⌒ SCENE TWO ⌒

# Grandmother's House

**Sign Walker #1:** Student walks across stage with the sign, "Thirty Years Earlier."

**Sign Walker #2:** Student walks across stage with the sign, "Grandmother's House."

**Little Red Riding Hood:** (*at grandmother's front door, knocking*) Grandma, it's me, Little Red Riding Hood! I've brought you some goodies from Gretel's cookie shop!

**Young Wolf:** (*pretending to be Grandmother*) Is that you, Little Red Riding Hood? Please come in!

**Little Red Riding Hood:** (*enters and walks toward "Grandma"*) Hello, Grandma! (*stops suddenly*) Wait, something's different about you.

**Young Wolf:** Why, whatever are you saying dear? Come. Sit down and show your old granny the goodies you brought her.

**Little Red:** Hmmmm. No, something is definitely different. Is it your eyes? Did you get contacts?

**Young Wolf:** (*patting the bed*) Come here dear.

**Little Red:** (*standing where she is*) Maybe it's your teeth. Is that new lipstick you're wearing?

**Young Wolf:** Come, come dear. Granny's very hungry.

**Little Red:** I know! It's your hair! You got a perm.

**Young Wolf:** Oh, for goodness sake. Take a better look. (*Wolf leans forward so Little Red can see better.*)

**Little Red:** Hey! You're not my grandma. You're a wolf!

**Young Wolf:** (*gets out of bed*) Finally. That's over!

**Little Red:** Back up buster! I have my cell phone set to call 911. What did you do with my grandma?

**Young Wolf:** Nothing. She was gone when I got here.

**Little Red:** So what are you doing here?

**Young Wolf:** (*pulls out a piece of paper*) Well, according to my job sheet, I am supposed to eat your grandma, dress up in her clothes, and then eat you when you show up.

**Little Red:** Your job sheet?

**Young Wolf:** It's a long story, kid.

**Little Red:** I have the time (*She sits on the bed next to the wolf, pulling out a cookie.*) Want a cookie?

**Young Wolf:** Thanks! I'm starving. You see, ever since I was a little pup, my parents have wanted me to join the Fraternal Order of Obnoxious and Devious Wolves or F.O.O.D. for short. My dad was a member when he was young and so was his dad. The F.O.O.D. wolves are those wolves you read about in all the papers. You know, the ones that eat little kids, blow down buildings, terrorize little pigs. I'm sure you've heard of them.

**Little Red:** Yes, I have. But you don't seem their type.

**Young Wolf:** Well, the truth is…(*there is a knock on the door*) Quick, hide me!

(*The wolf hides under the bed or someplace in the house.*)

**Little Red:** (*at door*) Well, hello. You're Grandma's neighbor, the woodcutter, right?

**Woodcutter:** Yes, I am. Your grandmother asked me to look in on the house while she was away in Florida. Everything okay? There's a wolf that's supposed to be wandering about.

**Little Red:** Everything is just fine, thank you.

**Woodcutter:** Are you sure? Your grandmother didn't say you'd be visiting while she was away. I could come in and check the place out for you.

**Little Red:** No, that's okay. Everything is fine. Here, have a cookie. Thanks again and goodbye! (*She closes the door and the wolf comes out of hiding.*)

**Young Wolf:** Whew! That was close! I think that's the same guy that left his two kids out in the woods not too long ago.

**Little Red:** No, you're thinking of Hansel and Gretel's father. He lives a few towns over. Now, please, continue your story.

**Young Wolf:** Well, I did join F.O.O.D. and somehow my boss found out that I used to babysit the little kids from my neighborhood. She thought that since I seemed to like little kids, I would enjoy eating one of them. And that's how I got this job. I do like kids, but not as food!

**Little Red:** Well, that's a relief.

**Young Wolf:** And now look what's happened. This was my first job and it's gotten all messed up. Do you know how much trouble I'm going to be in if any of the Fraternal Brothers find out what's happened? I'll be a disgrace to my entire profession! (*There is a knock at the door.*) Not again!

**Little Red:** Just a minute. (*at door*) Who is it?

**Goldilocks:** It's Goldilocks. Is that you Red?

**Little Red:** (*opening door*) Goldilocks! How are you? Run into any bears lately?

**Goldilocks:** Ha, ha, very funny. Actually, I'm selling cookies for my school so that we can buy more porridge-making equipment. Do you want to buy a few dozen? They're great!

**Little Red:** Well, my grandma isn't here right now and I don't have any money.

**Goldilocks:** (*sniffing*) Hey, what's that I smell? Do you have some porridge? It's been a long time since I've had any of that. (*She tries to see past Little Red into the house.*)

**Little Red:** You're probably just smelling the things I brought for Grandma.

**Goldilocks:** (*sniffing again*) No, it's not goodies. It actually smells like a bear or a wolf or something.

**Little Red:** Well, Grandma has been using a new perfume, you know, to help her smell more woodsy so that she can blend in to the forest surroundings. She sprays it everywhere. I'm sure that's what you're smelling. (*Goldilocks continues sniffing and trying to see around Little Red.*) Take care, and good luck on your cookie sales! See you later! (*She closes door and returns to the wolf.*)

**Young Wolf:** Whew! That was a little too close! I have to get out of here.

**Little Red:** Actually, I think I have an idea. You like little kids, right?

**Young Wolf:** It's a little embarrassing, me being a wolf and all. But yes, I do like little kids. There's something fun about being around them.

**Little Red:** And you don't like to eat them, right?

**Young Wolf:** (*makes a face*) Yuck! No! I've never been much of a meat eater.

**Little Red:** I think this just might work!

**Young Wolf:** What? What's your idea? (*They are interrupted by another bang on the door.*)

**Inspector Frank:** (*banging on the door*) Open up! It's Inspector Frank N. Furter, Private Investigator. (Wolf hides as Little Red goes to the door.)

**Little Red:** Let me see your badge please. (*Inspector Frank shows his badge under the door or through the peephole. Little Red opens door*) Yes, how may I help you?

**Inspector Frank:** Hello, Ma'am. I've been hired by the three little pigs to track down a big bad wolf, and I have reason to believe he may be here.

**Little Red:** Oh, no. There are no big bad wolves here. I just stopped by to drop off some cookies for Grandma. Would you like one?

**Inspector Frank:** No thanks, Ma'am, I'm on duty. Are you sure you haven't seen any big bad wolves around? They can be mighty dangerous.

**Little Red:** No, I'm sure. No wolves here. Uh-uh. No siree!

**Inspector Frank:** They've been known to eat people, you know.

**Little Red:** I know, but I have my cell phone with me and the woodcutter down the road already checked the place out.

**Inspector Frank:** Are you really sure? I mean completely positively sure? Because the three little pigs are going to be upset if I come home empty-handed, and I only get paid if I find a wolf.

**Little Red:** Well, I think I did see a wolf go that way (points) not too long ago. Maybe if you hurry you can still catch him.

**Inspector Frank:** Gee, thanks! (*He dashes off.*)

**Little Red:** (*closes door and turns back to wolf*) Okay, we don't have much time. Here, take this. (*She gives him the red item.*)

**Young Wolf:** What? Why?

**Little Red:** Go back to F.O.O.D. and tell them another wolf had already eaten me when you showed up. Tell them this (holding out the red item) was all that was left of me. Show it to them so they will believe your story. Then sneak away and find the next carriage to Albertville. My Uncle Yellow lives there. He's a teacher. I'll call him and have him meet you at the station.

**Young Wolf:** Wait. Slow down. What are you thinking of?

**Little Red:** I've got the perfect job for you, and it has nothing to do with eating little kids. Have you ever thought about being a kindergarten teacher?

**Young Wolf:** A teacher! Certainly, I've thought about it, but I'm a wolf and never in my wildest dreams did I think I'd even have a chance.

**Little Red:** Well, it is a lot of work, and the pay is lousy.

**Young Wolf:** That's okay. As long as I get to work with kids without having to eat them, I'd love it!

**Little Red:** Okay then, off you go. (pushes him out while dialing cell phone) Hi, Uncle Yellow, I've got the perfect someone who wants to learn how to be a teacher. He's energetic, clever, and is willing to work hard.

(*Little Red exits.*)

## ⌒ SCENE THREE ⌒

# Mr. Wolf's Classroom

**Sign Walker #3:** Student walks across stage with the sign, "Thirty Years Later"

**Sign Walker #4:** Student walks across stage with the sign, "Back in the Classroom of Mr. Wolf."

(*Classroom actors unfreeze.*)

**Wolf:** And that, children, is the story of how I became a teacher.

**Kids 1,2,3:** (*together*) Wow!

**Kid 1:** Did you ever see Little Red Riding Hood again?

**Wolf:** No, I never did. Although I heard she grew up to be a fine teacher herself.

**Kid 2:** Tell us another story!

**Kid 3:** Yeah, tell us about one of the other wolves, the ones that liked to eat little pigs.

**Wolf:** No, I'll tell you a story another day. Right now, it's time for recess. Everyone outside! (*Students exit noisily. Wolf pulls out the same red item Little Red gave him thirty years earlier.*) Well, Little Riding Hood (*to audience*), the wolf lived happily ever after.

# Language Arts Activity Page

## ❧ ACTIVITY ONE ❧

## For Hire—Jobs and Fairy Tales

### PERSUASIVE WRITING: Writing Persuasively About Self

The wolf never dreamed he had the right qualifications to be a teacher. It took some time and self-reflection for him to realize that he could enter the profession and do a good job. Let students reflect on their personal characteristics and use their ideas as material for persuasive writing.

Provide students with the yellow pages of a phone book or the classified section of a newspaper. Then encourage them to find three or four jobs they think would be interesting. Using The Perfect Match reproducible on page 41, instruct students to list adjectives that describe personal qualities they possess that they feel are also important for the job. Using this list as a reference, students can write a paragraph telling why they would be good for the job.

**Extend it!** Let students pair other fairy tale characters with jobs and write persuasively about why those jobs "fit" for those characters. For example, why would Goldilocks make the perfect banker or Pinocchio the perfect private investigator?

## ❧ ACTIVITY TWO ❧

## Cookies for Grandma

### DESCRIPTIVE WRITING: Using Sensory Details

At several points in this play, sensory details are important, such as when Goldilocks smells the wolf or when Little Red Riding Hood can't see that the wolf isn't her grandmother. Help students generate sensory details for their own writing by collecting sensory data from around your school.

Take brief field trips to the playground, the school library, the cafeteria (right before lunch), and the music room. Ask students to bring a notebook and collect information about what they see, smell, and hear. To help students organize information, use the Fabulous Five Senses Chart on page 17. Once students have collected at least three pieces of data for each sense, ask them to write a description of their school as their senses "see" it. Encourage students to include enough sensory detail so that someone who is unfamiliar with the school can experience it.

**Extend it!** Ask students to collect sensory data and write descriptions of other familiar places, such as their bedrooms, a mall, a church, or a playground. To further challenge students, ask them to collect data and write about locations as if they were missing one sense, such as hearing or sight.

## ❧ ACTIVITY THREE ❧

# A New Twist on an Old Tale

### NARRATIVE WRITING: Developing Perspective

What if, for all these years, the big bad wolf in fairy tales has really been misunderstood? This play certainly asks us to rethink our stereotype of the wolf.

Using the perspective of the wolf from the play, give students a chance to rewrite the traditional story of Little Red Riding Hood, in which the wolf is a good character and not a bad one. You may wish to read *The True Story of The Three Little Pigs*, by Jon Scieszka, as a reference point. Hold a class discussion to help students think of ideas as to how and why the wolf has been misunderstood. Students may wish to write this story in a first-person narrative.

**Extend it!** Let students pick other "misunderstood" fairy-tale characters and rewrite traditional stories from their perspectives. Characters to include may be: Cinderella's evil stepsisters or stepmother, the wolf in the three little pigs tale, the witch from "Hansel and Gretel," Rapunzel's evil queen mother, or the queen from "Snow White."

Name_____ Date_____

# The Perfect Match

Could the Big Bad Wolf really become a great kindergarten teacher?

What's your dream job? What skills and personal qualities does a person need to have to succeed at this job? Fill out the job description below to describe your dream job and the skills and personal qualities you're going to work on to become a real professional!

**Hint:** *Check the classified section of newspaper for an ad about your job to see what kinds of qualifications you might need!*

**Job:** _____ **My position/ title:** _____

**Important skills for this job:**

- _____
- _____
- _____
- _____
- _____

**Skills:** typing, organizing, calculating, planning, singing, dancing, translating, speaking another language, drawing, presenting, designing, training in a sport, training in a trade

**Important personal qualities for this job:**

- _____
- _____
- _____
- _____
- _____

**Personal qualities:** cooperative, aggressive, quick, thoughtful, organized, punctual, energetic, imaginative, verbal, dexterous, critical, daring, cautious, ambitious, hard-working, dedicated, creative, adventurous, reliable, smart, resourceful

**What I'd do in a typical work day:**

_____

_____

_____

_____

**Why I'd be perfect for this job:**

_____

_____

_____

_____

# LIVE: It's Fairy Tale News!

## Getting Started!

## Introduction

Your students step into the role of reporter in this play and discover the news from a different angle as it unfolds in twists on classic fairy tales. After reading this play, students will never look at the news (and fairy tales) the same way again.

### Costume Ideas

**Anchors (Pete and Ruby):** fairy-tale attire or suits and headsets. They can carry coffee cups and papers.

**Field Reporters:** dress for their particular assignment. (Gore May can wear a chef's hat and an apron and carry a bowl and a spoon. Katie Lean can wear a sports outfit.) They may also carry press identification badges and hold microphones.

### Set Ideas

The two anchors remain seated or standing throughout the play. You may wish to have a sign hanging behind them (FT NEWS, for Fairy Tale News) and **living props** that include camera operators who aim cardboard cameras at the anchors or the field reporters on the scene. Characters being interviewed may get in place quietly before their segments or may enter as their segments begin.

The Sleeping Beauty segment may be elaborate with "castle" implements, or may be simple with a bed and a chair. The Gore May segment can include a backdrop of a brick wall with a mailbox and characters dressed as chefs holding jars of "spaghetti sauce." For the Jack in the Beanstalk segment you may wish to include a beanstalk made of construction paper or papier maché–covered wrapping paper tubes with protestors holding signs ("Save the Sprout," "Malls Mean Jobs") and megaphones.

## THE CAST

- ⚭ Ruby Red
- ⚭ Pete Charming
- ⚭ Wanda Whereabout
- ⚭ Gore May
- ⚭ Hasket Hansen
- ⚭ Katie Lean
- ⚭⚭ Sleeping Beauty
- ⚭⚭ David Dashing
- ⚭⚭ Pig 1
- ⚭⚭ Pig 2
- ⚭⚭ Pig 3
- ⚭⚭ Jack
- ⚭⚭ Barbara Lou
- ⚭⚭ Rumpelstiltskin
- ⚭⚭ Protestor #1
- ⚭⚭⚭ Wolf
- ⚭⚭⚭ Protestors (4–5)
- ⚭⚭⚭ Elsie

⚭ *Role with challenging speaking part*

⚭⚭ *Role with fewer lines*

⚭⚭⚭ *Nonspeaking part or part with few words which may be appropriate for students with limited English proficiency or with special needs.*

42

# LIVE: It's Fairy Tale News!

## The Script!

Ruby Red

Pete Charming

### The Cast

| | | |
|---|---|---|
| Ruby Red | Little Pig 2 | Protester #1 |
| Pete Charming | Wolf | Protestors (4–5) |
| Wanda Whereabout | Little Pig 3 | Katie Lean |
| David Dashing | Hasket Hansen | L. Mermaid |
| Sleeping Beauty | Barbara Lou | Rumpelstiltskin |
| Gore May | Jack | |
| Little Pig 1 | Elsie | |

(*Anchors are seated or stand in place.*)

**Ruby Red:** (*to audience or camera*) Hello and good evening. I am Ruby Red and this is a special edition of the Fairy Tales News at your local FT News Station. Our top story tonight takes place high in the tower of a castle where a young beauty has just awoken. (looks at Pete) Pete?

**Pete Charming:** (*to audience or camera*) Yes, hello everyone. I'm Pete Charming. Now we turn to our investigative reporter, Wanda Whereabout, to get the latest about this once-in-a-hundred-years event. Wanda? (Pete and Ruby turn to look at Wanda, who is with Sleeping Beauty and David Dashing.)

**Wanda:** (*to audience or camera*) Hello Ruby. Hello Pete. This is Wanda Whereabout reporting live from the Rose Tower Castle. I am here with Sleeping Beauty and David Dashing with some astonishing news. David, can you tell the audience what has just happened?

**David:** Sure, Wanda. (*grabs the microphone*) I just lost a tooth!!! (He smiles and points at his mouth for the camera to see.)

**Wanda:** No, David. (*points to Sleeping Beauty*) I mean, what just happened with her?

**David:** Oh yeah, well this morning my mom sent me out to get some exercise, and I thought it would be really cool to climb some stairs, so I climbed this tower and found this lady here sleeping in a bed with a sign that said "Kiss me." But I've heard that sometimes if you kiss people on the lips they're really frogs in disguise, and I think kissing is really icky anyway...But the sign did say, "Kiss me," so I decided to kiss her hand and see what happened. But it wasn't anything exciting. She just woke up. Did I show you that I lost a tooth?

**Wanda:** (*ignoring the tooth comment from David*) Sleeping Beauty, how does it feel to be awake after all these years?

**Sleeping Beauty:** (*yawning*) Exhausting! I was right in the middle of the perfect dream when I woke up to see this little kid I don't even know right next to my bed.

**Wanda:** So, when are you two getting married?

**Sleeping Beauty
and David:** (*together*) What?

**David:** I'm only nine.

**Sleeping Beauty:** I don't even know him.

**Wanda:** Oh, I've heard royal weddings are just wonderful. Who do you think will do the flowers for you?

**David:** I'm allergic to flowers.

**Sleeping Beauty:** (*pointing to David*) He's only nine.

**Wanda:** And the food! Do you know that our news station covered Cinderella's wedding? The cake was just fabulous! Have you two picked out your cake yet?

**David:** I love cake. But just the frosting part.

**Sleeping Beauty:** What news station did you say you were from? And what kind of reporter are you, anyway? Things have certainly changed while I've been asleep!

**Wanda:** Just one final question, and then I will leave you two alone to plan your wedding: Do either of you have any thoughts about your honeymoon?

**David:** Oh, I've never been to the moon before. Cool!

**Sleeping Beauty:** This is ridiculous. I'm going back to sleep. (*She closes her eyes and snores.*)

**Wanda:** (*smiling back toward the camera or audience*) Well, Ruby and Peter, another love story ends happily. This is Wanda Whereabout reporting live from the Rose Tower Castle.

**Pete:** (*to audience or camera*) Oh, young love! It's so wonderful!

**Ruby:** (*to audience or camera*) It is, Pete! And now we turn to our cooking segment. Tonight we have a special treat. Our very own

Fairy Tale News channel chef, Gore May, is on site at the house of the three little pigs. Ms. May?

**Gore May:** Hi, Ruby and Pete! Today on our cooking segment we are going to discuss Italian cooking with the three little pigs. I am here with them after their recent narrow escape from the wolf, and it seems this experience has helped them learn quite a bit about cooking. (*to Little Pig 1*) Little Pig, can you tell the audience about the special sauce you have recently prepared?

**Little Pig 1:** Yes, Ms. May. As you know, we had to create a fire to prevent that big old bad wolf from coming down our chimney. That's when we discovered that if you keep spaghetti sauce over the fire and cook it slowly for many days it tastes much better.

**Gore May:** Yum. It does look good. (*to Little Pig 2*) Little Pig, tell us what you added to this special sauce?

**Little Pig 2:** Well, you see, my first house was made of sticks from the Enchanted Forest, and when the wolf blew it down, a few of those sticks got mixed in with this sauce. That became our special ingredient.

**Gore May:** And I understand these enchanted sticks come from a secret place that you can't reveal?

**Little Pig 2:** That's right, ma'am. They are very hard to get.

(*Enter wolf, unnoticed by others. Wolf begins pantomiming huffing and puffing.*)

**Gore May:** (*to Little Pig 3*) Now, Little Pig, I understand that you are in charge of selling this sauce?

**Little Pig 3:** Yes, I am. (*notices wind*) Wow! Isn't it a little windy all of a sudden?

**Gore May:** Oh my, you're right, where did that wind come from? It was supposed to be clear today. (*Wolf continues pantomime blowing.*)

**Little Pig 2:** I have to get home. My new house isn't insured! (*He exits.*)

**Gore May:** No, wait!

**Little Pig 3:** Oh, no! I have to save my new house too!

**Gore May:** No, really. I'm sure it's just a little breeze.

**Little Pig 1:** This seems a little too familiar. I'm out of here! (*He exits.*)

**Gore May:** (*to camera or audience*) Well, I guess that's our show for today. Back to you, Pete and Ruby!

**Ruby:** (*to audience or camera*) Yes. Well, Pete, a protest has broken out at the house of Jack, where Jack lives with his mother and Elsie, the famous cow who was sold for magic beans.

**Pete:** (*to audience or camera*) Yes, Ruby, it does look serious. Apparently, Jack's beanstalk, which made history just a few years ago, is scheduled to be chopped down to make room for a new shopping mall. Things are sprouting up fast over this issue. We now turn to Hasket Hanson for an on-the-spot report.

**Hasket:** (*to audience or camera*) Yes, Pete. I am here at the spot of the protest with Barbara Lou, Jack's mother. (*to Barbara Lou*) Barbara Lou, can you tell us what's happening here?

**Barbara Lou:** I most certainly can! I told my son not to get involved with those magic beans. I told him they were nothing but trouble. But he didn't listen. And now look! (*She points to the protesters.*)

**Hasket:** (*turning to Jack*) Jack, tell us how you feel about all this.

**Jack:** Feel? How do you think I feel? My mom's mad at me. The giant's mad at me. Elsie's even mad at me. And you want to know how I feel? Hmmph! (*He crosses his arms and turns away.*)

**Hasket:** (*to Elsie*) Elsie, do you have any thoughts on the situation?

**Elsie:** Moo. Moo. Moo…

**Hasket:** (*to Protester #1*) You're here protesting this situation. Can you tell us why you are doing this?

**Protester #1:** Yes, sir! Make sure you get my good side for the camera. We are here because we believe the beanstalk has become a valuable part of our landscape. It has provided shade for the park nearby and has become a tourist attraction for our little town. And now, they want to tear it down. To build a mall! (*waves at camera*) Hi, Mom!

**Hasket:** (*to audience or camera*) Well, Pete and Ruby, we'll have to wait and see if this situation grows into something giant. This is Hasket Hansen reporting live from the house of Jack and his beanstalk. Back to you at the main desk. (*Actors exit quietly.*)

**Pete:** Thanks, Hasket. And now on to sports. (*He turns to Katie Lean. L. Mermaid is sitting in a chair next to her.*)

**Katie Lean:** (*to audience or camera*) Hi, folks! I'm Katie Lean with sports, and today it looks as if another historic moment is being made by one of our very own citizens. Joining us in our studio today is Ms. L. Mermaid. (*L. Mermaid enters*) Ms. Mermaid, please tell us your exciting news.

**L. Mermaid:** Well, Katie, I just got word that my little guppy synchronized-swimming team will be heading to the Olympics.

**Katie Lean:** Congratulations. Everyone knows how hard you worked after the loss of your singing career.

**L. Mermaid:** Yes, but I think I've found my new career. Those little guppies are so wonderful to school.

**Katie Lean:** Maybe later you can show us some moves in our tidal pool out back. Thank you for stopping by! (*L. Mermaid stands, they shake hands, and she exits. Katie continues.*) In other sports news, the dance marathon involving the twelve princesses continues into the night. This is its fourth night, and although shoes have been

wearing out, not one princess has given up yet. And now, for our second guest, we have The-Spinner-Formerly-Known-As-Rumpelstiltskin, joining us by satellite phone, where he has been a participant in the world class gold-spinning contest. Are you there Spinner?

**Rumpelstiltskin:** (*off stage*) Yes, I am here, Katie.

**Katie Lean:** Well, I hear that you are in first-place so far in the amount of straw that has been spun into gold.

**Rumpelstiltskin:** You got it! Gold's the game down here!

**Katie Lean:** And has anyone guessed your name?

**Rumpelstiltskin:** Actually, everyone down here is so busy spinning gold that they don't really care what my new name is. It's very refreshing just to come here and compete doing something I love.

**Kate Lean:** Well, we wish you the best of luck. That's it for sports. Back to you, Pete.

**Pete:** Thanks, Katie. That concludes our evening segment of the Fairy Tale News. Tune in tomorrow to find out about the new day-care center being opened by Rumpelstiltskin. Also, make sure to watch for a touching interview with the wicked witch of the Northeast on how she is coping after losing her only pair of magic garnet slippers.

**Ruby:** And in our cooking segment, Gore May will show you how to make a delicious apple pie using the enchanted apples from Snow White's apple orchard. Also, we will give you an update on the hunt for the land's most-wanted burglary suspect, Goldilocks.

**Pete:** Goodnight and happily ever after!

# Language Arts Activity Page

## ❧ ACTIVITY ONE ❧

## The Fairy Tale Tribune

### EXPOSITORY WRITING: Writing about the main idea

Television is just one way members of the fairy-tale community receive news and information. Let your students use their imaginations and practice creating written news about the fairy-tale community through a classroom fairy-tale newspaper. Students may be creative in their articles, but remind them they must include the five W's (who, what, where, when, and why) in the lead paragraph.

Ask students to brainstorm fairy-tale events (either from the play or from fairy tales in general.) The News Article Planner on page 52 can serve as a template for helping students structure their stories once they are ready to start writing. You may wish to compile articles into a format that looks like a newspaper and distribute this as a classroom issue of "The Fairy Tale Times."

Extend it! Students can create other parts of a newspaper, such as an opinion section (where students may write for or against the demolition of the beanstalk, for example), want ads, commercial advertisements, and fairy-tale recipes.

## ❧ ACTIVITY TWO ❧

## And Now, a Word from Our Sponsor

### PERSUASIVE WRITING: Creating and Developing a Persuasive Argument

Give your students practice developing persuasive arguments by letting them imagine what kinds of commercials might appear during a fairy-tale news broadcast. Cinderella may advertise a new kind of unbreakable glass slipper, for example, or Rapunzel may be an infomercial spokesperson for hair products.

Begin by having students brainstorm lists of fairy-tale characters and specific items they are associated with, such as Snow White and apples, Cinderella and time or shoes, Rapunzel and hair products, and Rumpelstiltskin and gold.

Advertisements may take two forms: ads that sell products developed by fairy-tale characters themselves (for example, Jack's beans and Sleeping Beauty's orthopedic mattresses) or ads that sell things fairy-tale characters may need (such as a beeper to

keep Cinderella on time at the ball or a cell phone for the pigs to use to call for help when they meet up with the wolf).

After choosing a product idea, students must think of at least three reasons why a person would want to buy the product and develop a poster, magazine print ad, infomercial script, or television commercial ad. Provide examples for students to read, listen to, or watch.

**Extend it!** Challenge students to develop an advertisement for the same product in two different formats. Encourage discussion and comparison of how different media present the same information.

### ❧ ACTIVITY THREE ❧

# Lights, Camera, Action!

### NARRATIVE WRITING: Creating dialogue

Even though the play ends, the news in the lives of the fairy-tale characters doesn't. Give students the chance to practice creating dialogue as they interview fairy-tale characters in this activity.

To begin, students brainstorm fairy-tale news items they wish to report. These items can be from any fairy tale and not just situations found in the play. They may include such things as the moment Snow White bites the poison apple, the time when Pinocchio becomes a real boy, or an hour after Hansel and Gretel have escaped the witch.

Next, instruct students to recreate this moment in the form of a dialogue, using the form of the play as an example. Students should write both as the reporter and as the character being interviewed. They may even wish to write as themselves. Focus on allowing students to practice using conversation and dialogue as a way to relay information. If you wish, you may ask students, after their script dialogues are complete, to change them into narrative dialogue form, such as the kind found in stories, complete with quotation marks and proper punctuation.

**Extend it!** Let students perform and videotape or audiotape their own dialogue news scripts. If your school has an all-school video system, news segments can be played so the whole school can enjoy them. In addition, students may also wish to create a dialogue for a fairy-tale soap opera or radio show, complete with sound effects.

Name_____ Date_____

# News Article Planner

Plan a front-page article for "The Fairy Tale Times!"
Select a fairy-tale character and an event to write
about. Brainstorm answers to the 5 W's and use that
information
to write a
terrific lead.
Finish the
article and
write a
catchy title.

**What's a lead?** A lead is the
sentence or sentences that kick-off
an article. It is packed with
information that gives a quick
summary of the event. Practice lead
writing by using the 5 W's.

### 5-W's Lead Planner

**1.** Who was involved?

**2.** What happened?

**3.** Where did it happen?

**4.** When did it happen?

**5.** Why did it happen?

_____

(your title)

by _____

(your name)

# Once Upon a Hundred-Years' Nap

## Introduction

Sleeping Beauty and the prince live happily in their castle. That is, until the prince's mother temporarily moves in and discovers her son and daughter-in-law don't exactly live the rich and royal lifestyle typical of fairy-tale couples. When she tries to lend a helping hand in this play, things become both disastrous and humorous.

### Costume Ideas

**Mr. Roberts:** neat white-collared shirt, slicked hair, a "mustache." He might sport white gloves and carry a tray.

**Jules:** large rubber cleaning gloves and an apron. She might carry a feather duster, dust rag, or small vacuum cleaner.

**Merrywell Charming:** costume jewelry, a tiara, long gloves, rings on all fingers. She might carry a stuffed dog or cat. (Merrywell's Helpers may carry large, empty boxes, pieces of actual luggage, animal cages, purses, or coats.)

### Set Ideas

There are two basic sets for this play: a breakfast room or dining room set and a living room set. The breakfast room set may be simple, with two chairs facing each other, or it may be more elaborate, with a table, a clock, a centerpiece, place settings, china, and even a "window" on the wall.

The living room set may also be very simple, with nothing more than chairs, or it may be elaborate, with furniture, a TV (made out of a box), pictures, or other things commonly found in a living room.

The opening and ending scenes call for a phone, which may be a toy plastic phone or an actual phone. Actors may also pantomime using a phone.

### THE CAST

- ⚜ Sleeping Beauty
- ⚜ Prince Stuart Charming
- ⚜ Merrywell Charming
- ⚜ Mr. Roberts, the butler
- ⚜⚜ Jules, the maid
- ⚜⚜ Daisy, the witch
- ⚜⚜ Marc Cedes
- ⚜⚜ Police Officer #1
- ⚜⚜ Police Officer #2
- ⚜⚜⚜ Sandy Man
- ⚜⚜⚜ Sign Walker #1
- ⚜⚜⚜ Sign Walker #2
- ⚜⚜⚜ Sign Walker #3
- ⚜⚜⚜ Sign Walker #4
- ⚜⚜⚜ Sign Walker #5
- ⚜⚜⚜ Merrywell Charming's luggage handlers (2–6)

⚜ *Role with challenging speaking part*

⚜⚜ *Role with fewer lines*

⚜⚜⚜ *Nonspeaking part or part with few words which may be appropriate for students with limited English proficiency or with special needs.*

# Once Upon a Hundred-Years' Nap

## The Script!

## The Cast

| | |
|---|---|
| Sign Walker #1 | Sign Walker #3 |
| Sleeping Beauty | Marc Cedes |
| Prince Stuart Charming | Police Officer #1 |
| Mr. Roberts, the butler | Police Officer #2 |
| Sign Walker #2 | Sandy Mann |
| Jules, the maid | Daisy, the witch |
| Merrywell Charming | Sign Walker #4 |
| Merrywell Charming's luggage handlers (2–6) | Sign Walker #5 |

# Breakfast in the Castle

*(Sleeping Beauty and Prince Stuart Charming are on-stage eating breakfast.)*

**Sign Walker #1:** Walks across stage holding sign, "Scene I: Breakfast at Sleeping Beauty's Castle."

**Sleeping Beauty:** Good morning, Prince Stuart, how are you? Did you sleep well on your new mattress?

**Prince Stuart Charming:** Oh, Sleeping Beauty, it was great! I am so proud of you! The new mattresses you've invented are going to help children everywhere get a good night's sleep.

**Sleeping Beauty:** Well, after spending a hundred years asleep on that old uncomfortable mattress, I knew I had to do something. It's so nice to have a husband who is supportive of my ideas!

**Prince Stuart Charming:** Well, your mattress invention is going to be a hit. I can't wait for you to open your first factory. Is it going to be soon?

**Sleeping Beauty:** I have a meeting with the Sandman tomorrow to talk about the details. (*Mr. Roberts enters.*)

**Mr. Roberts:** Mister Prince Stuart, the phone is for you. (*hands Prince Stuart Charming the phone*) I believe it is your mother.

**Prince Stuart Charming:** (*taking phone*) Hello, mother. Yes? Well...I...Sure. When? Uh, okay. (*He hangs up the phone and gives it to Mr. Roberts.*)

**Sleeping Beauty:** Well?

**Prince Stuart Charming:** Have I told you what a wonderful wife you are?

**Sleeping Beauty:** Yes, three times already today. What did your mother say?

**Prince Stuart Charming:** Do you know that being asleep for a hundred years only made you more beautiful?

**Sleeping Beauty:** What did your mother say?

**Prince Stuart Charming:** And how about the weather outside? Hasn't it been lovely lately? I was thinking we could walk over to Snow White's apple orchard and…

**Sleeping Beauty:** Stuart Charming, why did your mother call?

**Prince Stuart Charming:** (*fast, in one breath*) Well, it seems her castle is being remodeled and the fumes are getting to be really bad from all the gold paint they are using and you know how delicate mother is and she needs a place to stay and it will just be for a few weeks and you know how I can't say no to her and…

**Sleeping Beauty:** (*interrupting*) It's okay, Stuart. I'm sure it can't be that bad. We'll have Jules make up the guest quarters in the new castle wing.

**Prince Stuart Charming:** You are so wonderful.

**Sleeping Beauty:** I know.

**Prince Stuart Charming:** It will only be for a few weeks. I promise.

(*All exit.*)

## ⌒ SCENE TWO ⌒

# That Afternoon in the Castle

**Sign Walker #2:** Walks across stage with the sign, "Scene 2: That Afternoon in the Castle."

(*Sleeping Beauty and Prince Stuart Charming. Sleeping Beauty holds a note pad and checks off items as she talks with the other characters.*)

**Maid Jules:** (*enters*) Mr. and Mrs. Charming, I made up the spare castle quarters for Mr. Charming's mother. Is there anything else you need me to do?

**Prince Stuart Charming:** Thank you, Jules. Now, did you remember to move the bed the way mother likes it?

**Maid Jules:** Yes. I put it so that one corner is facing northeast, and it is no more than two inches away from the window.

**Sleeping Beauty:** And did you fill a pitcher of drinking water and make sure it was exactly 56.3 degrees? Merrywell Charming must have her water at just the right temperature, you know.

**Maid Jules:** Yes, and I also remembered to empty the spare room down the hall so she will have a place for all her luggage. I haven't forgotten what happened last time.

**Sleeping Beauty:** Oh, Jules, you are a gem!

**Prince Stuart Charming:** This will just be for a few weeks. I promise.

**Sleeping Beauty:** And we'll make sure you get a long vacation afterward.

*(Mr. Roberts enters, followed by Merrywell Charming and her helpers. Each helper carries a piece of luggage or box.)*

**Mr. Roberts:** (*to Sleeping Beauty and Prince Stuart Charming*) Madam and sir, Mrs. Merrywell Charming is here.

**Merrywell Charming:** (*to Prince Stuart Charming*) Darling! How is my little baby boy? Are you eating your vegetables? Are you getting enough sleep? Are you still wearing the pajamas Auntie Gerta made you?

**Sleeping Beauty:** Hello, Mother Charming.

**Merrywell Charming:** (*to Sleeping Beauty*) Oh. Hello, dear. It's good to see you. (*turns back to Stuart*) Now Stuart, these next few weeks are going to be so much fun. You just sit back and relax and let Mommy do everything for you. (*She leads him off stage and is followed by her helpers.*)

**Prince Stuart Charming:** (*being led away, looks back at Sleeping Beauty, and mouths HELP!*)

*(Remaining actors exit.)*

## ꕥ SCENE THREE ꕥ

# The Castle, The Next Morning

**Sign Walker #3:** Walks across the stage with the sign, "The Castle: The Next Morning."

*(Sleeping Beauty, Prince Stuart Charming, and Merrywell Charming sit and eat breakfast.)*

**Merrywell Charming:** *(to Stuart)* Now Stuart, today Mommy is going to watch the servants and make sure all your prince outfits are nice and clean. You have that ball to attend next week, remember?

**Prince Stuart Charming:** Well, actually, mother, I have been washing my own clothes.

**Merrywell Charming:** WHAT?! How long has this been going on?

**Prince Stuart Charming:** Oh...for awhile.

**Merrywell Charming:** But...But...What about your castle laundry person?

**Sleeping Beauty:** Well, she retired shortly after we got married and we just never got around to hiring another one.

**Merrywell Charming:** But you two can't do your own laundry. No prince ever does his own laundry. It's simply not done! What will the neighbors think?

**Sleeping Beauty:** Really, it's okay.

*(Marc Cedes enters.)*

**Marc Cedes:** Well, Mr. and Mrs. Charming, I'm off to Hawaii. I sure appreciate the vacation!

**Merrywell Charming:** *(to Marc)* Who are you?

**Marc Cedes:** I'm the coach driver for the Charmings, ma'am. Name's Marc Cedes *(sticks out a hand)* Pleased to meet you! *(to Prince Stuart Charming and Sleeping Beauty)* Thanks again! *(He exits.)*

**Merrywell Charming:** Please tell me you have another driver filling in while Mr. Cedes is on vacation.

**Sleeping Beauty:** Well, actually, I learned how to drive the coach awhile ago and…

**Merrywell Charming:** Oh no, no, no, this just won't do. This just isn't done by royalty. Listen. You two don't worry. I'll take care of everything. (*starts exiting, muttering*) Imagine, washing your own clothes. Driving your own coach. Oh no, no, no.

**Sleeping Beauty:** I suppose we shouldn't tell her that sometimes we give the cook the weekend off and we cook for ourselves too.

**Prince Stuart Charming:** No, I think the shock would be too much.

(*Police officers 1 and 2 rush into the room, followed by Mr. Roberts.*)

**Police Officer 1:** (*loudly*) Okay, everyone just freeze!

**Prince Stuart Charming and Sleeping Beauty:** (*together*) What?!

**Police Officer #2:** Where's the emergency? We got a 911 call that someone needed help.

**Mr. Roberts:** I tried to tell them everything was fine but they insisted on coming in.

**Prince Stuart Charming:** Will someone tell me what is going on?

**Police Officer #1:** Some lady called and said her son needed help.

**Prince Stuart Charming:** Uh-oh.

**Sleeping Beauty:** (*to Stuart*) Your mother called 911? Because you are doing your own laundry and I am driving our coach? (*to Mr. Roberts*) Mr. Roberts, will you please take these nice gentlemen to the front room and explain the situation.

**Mr. Roberts:** (*sighs*) Very well, ma'am. (*Mr. Roberts and the two police officers leave.*)

**Sleeping Beauty:** Stuart?

**Prince Stuart Charming:** I know, I know. I'll talk to her. (*Stuart exits off-stage.*)

**Mr. Roberts:** (*returning, followed by the Sandman*):  Ms. Charming? A Mr. Sandy Mann is here to see you.

**Sleeping Beauty:** Oh, hello, Sandy. How are you? I am so excited to tell you about my new mattresses.

**Sandy Mann:** Yes, yes, Sleeping Beauty. I can hardly wait to see what you have planned. I knew you were just the one for this business with your previous sleeping experience.

**Sleeping Beauty:** Well let's go into the living room where we can talk. Mr. Roberts, please show Sandy our living room. I am going to go make some tea. (*She exits with Sandy Mann.*)

## ◠ SCENE FOUR ◠

# The Castle Living Room

**Sign Walker #4:** Walks across stage holding sign, "The Castle Living Room: The Same Day."

(*Daisy is seated in the drawing room. Sleeping Beauty enters with a cup.*)

**Sleeping Beauty:** Here you go Sandy, here's your tea. (*to Daisy*) Who are you?

**Daisy:** Oh, thank you. Tea would be lovely right now.

**Sleeping Beauty:** Uh, okay. But who are you? And where is Sandy?

**Daisy:** (*taking tea and sipping it*) Oh that funny little man? He's over there.

**Sleeping Beauty:** (*stepping over to where Daisy points*) What? Where? There's nothing here but sand. And again, you are?

**Daisy:** (*standing*) The name's Daisy. Daisy White. Here's my card. My specialty is helping out with domestic situations. Merrywell Charming hired me to help out around the place.

**Sleeping Beauty:** Hmmmm. Your name sounds familiar. Didn't you used to be Snow White's stepmother or something?

**Daisy:** It was a tragedy really, that whole mirror thing. I was so misunderstood by everyone. The media was just terrible!

**Sleeping Beauty:** Uh, okay. But where is my friend Sandy? He was here just a minute ago.

**Daisy:** I already told you. He's over there. (*pointing*)

**Sleeping Beauty:** But there's nothing there but a pile of sand...Oh no. Wait. You didn't. Did you turn the sandman into...into...sand???

**Daisy:** Well it couldn't be helped. He was most uncooperative and, after all, I was hired to help.

**Sleeping Beauty:** (*yelling*) Mr. Roberts! Mr. Roberts! Come here please! (*Mr. Roberts enters on all fours.*)

**Mr. Roberts:** Meow, meow, meow.

**Daisy:** Did I mention that Mr. Roberts was also being most uncooperative?

**Sleeping Beauty:** (*petting Mr. Roberts*) You mean this cat is Mr. Roberts?

**Daisy:** I heard you had a mouse problem.

**Sleeping Beauty:** (*yelling*) Stuart Charming, get in here right now! (*Stuart rushes in.*)

**Stuart:** Yes, yes, what's wrong? (*to cat*) Oh, nice kitty. Is it a stray?

**Sleeping Beauty:** No, that would be our poor butler, Mr. Roberts. And that (*pointing*) is my friend Sandy Mann. And this (*pointing*) is Daisy, Snow White's former stepmother, who has been hired by YOUR mother to take care of things around here.

**Stuart:** Oh.

**Sleeping Beauty:** Now this is what is going to happen. I am going to leave this room and the next time I come back, everything is going to be the way it was. Sandy is going to be the sandman again, instead of a pile of sand. Mr. Roberts is going to be our butler again, instead of a cat. (*Jules jumps in, interrupting.*)

**Jules:** Ribbit, ribbit.

**Sleeping Beauty:** (*to Daisy*) I'm afraid to ask why there is a frog in our house.

**Daisy:** You had a most uncooperative maid.

**Sleeping Beauty:** (*to Stuart*) Our maid, Jules, is going to be our maid again, instead of a frog. (*to Daisy*) Are there any other animals wandering about our castle that I should know about?

**Daisy:** You might want to ignore the fire-breathing dragon outside near the moat.

**Sleeping Beauty:** (*to Stuart*) And this, this, Daisy person will be gone and everything will be back to normal!

**Prince Stuart Charming:** Of course, of course.

(*Merrywell Charming enters.*)

**Merrywell Charming:** Great news everyone! I've been asked to be on that television show, "Lifestyles of the Fairly Famous." I know this is short notice and I do hope it is okay but they need me to fly out right away. It's going to be filmed in Hawaii! Oh, do you know how jealous the neighbors will be? Do you know how many parties I will get invited to after this? Ta ta, now. Stuart, don't forget to eat your vegetables, and Sleeping Beauty do take care. Daisy, come with me. I need you on the set! (*Merrywell exits and Daisy follows.*)

**Sleeping Beauty:** (*Grabbing Daisy*) Wait just a minute! You have a few things to change back before you leave.

**Daisy:** (*sighs, takes out a book, and starts to flip through it*) Oh all right! Just be warned: I don't reverse spells much—kindness was never in my nature. Hmmmm, let me think of where I might find the right incantation for the cat…Do you have a mirror?

*(Sleeping Beauty rolls her eyes and Prince Charming buries his head in his hands. Actors freeze.)*

### ⌒ SCENE FIVE ⌒

# The Castle, The Next Morning

**Sign Walker #5:** Walks across stage with sign, "The Castle: The Next Morning."

*(Sleeping Beauty and Prince Stuart Charming are at breakfast. Mr. Roberts enters, preening his forearms, cat-like.)*

**Prince Stuart Charming:** Good morning, Mr. Roberts. How are you this morning?

**Mr. Roberts:** Quite well, thank you, Mr. Charming, except that I have a strong craving for fish.

**Sleeping Beauty:** That should wear off in a few days. Is everything else okay?

**Mr. Roberts:** Well, we have had to keep Mistress Jules from eating all the flies and crickets in the garden. But other than that, things are almost back to normal.

**Prince Stuart Charming:** Everyone gets a nice long vacation, starting now. I promise!

*(Jules enters with phone.)*

**Jules:** Mr. Charming, the phone is for you. I believe it is your brother.

**Sleeping Beauty:** The one who raises poisonous fire-breathing toads as pets?

**Prince Stuart Charming:** *(takes phone)* Hello, Douglas…. The toads what?… Your castle burned down?… You have no place to stay?…

**Mr. Roberts, Jules, and Sleeping Beauty:** *(together)* Oh no!

# Language Arts Activity Page

## Curtain Call!

### ❧ ACTIVITY ONE ❧

## Just The Facts, Ma'am

**EXPOSITORY WRITING: Organizing and relaying factual information**

Even though the police were certainly not needed at the Charming household, they most likely had to file a report about their visit, describing in detail why they were called. Let students practice organizing and prioritizing information in this exercise by creating their own paragraphs of details.

Begin by asking students to make a list of everything that was amiss in the Charming castle. For example, the butler was turned into a cat, the maid was turned into a frog, Merrywell hired a witch to "help out," Sandy Mann was turned into sand, and Douglas called to say he'd like to visit with his poisonous pet toads.

After students have a list, instruct them to choose three of their favorite situations and write one paragraph for each, relaying the situation with a detailed account of the problems it will (or did) cause. You may also wish to ask students to write a paragraph describing solutions to each of the problems.

**Extend it!** Ask students to write an actual police report, either describing why the police were called to the castle or about any other situations from their lists. Students may also brainstorm and write reports for fairy-tale incidents not in the play (Goldilocks' burglary report, Big Bad Wolf's vandalism report, and so forth.)

### ❧ ACTIVITY TWO ❧

## Be My Guest

**DESCRIPTIVE WRITING: Character traits as supporting details**

There were many interesting characters in this play. Invite students to imagine, for a moment, that one of those characters moved in with them for a week. Ask them who would they most want to be their houseguests? Let students decide for themselves and relay this information through descriptive writing in this activity.

Begin by instructing students to pick a character they would like as a houseguest and list three reasons why they chose that character, as well as three things they would do with the character. For example, they may wish for Merrywell to come live with them because she would bring them lots of presents, or for Sleeping Beauty to visit because

she has made a good mattress and they will get a good night's sleep.

Next, ask students to write a page describing their characters, including as many character traits as they can. On this page, students should also include why they chose this character and the activities they will do together that week.

For contrast, you may also wish to have students write a description of someone who they would least like as their houseguest and details of what might happen if that person came to visit.

### ✤ ACTIVITY THREE ✤

# The Saga Continues...

### NARRATIVE WRITING: Perspective and point of view

At the end of this play, it sounds as if the adventures of the Charmings and their relatives are certain to continue. Give your students the chance to continue the Charming (or any other fairy-tale) adventure on their own and to practice writing from different perspectives.

First, encourage students to brainstorm ways to continue the fairy tale where the story leaves off. They can use the What Happens After "Happily Ever After"? reproducible (page 66) to organize their ideas. You might use the reproducible on the overhead and model how to fill it out, prompting students to offer creative answers to questions such as "What problems might happen when Douglas and his poisonous, fire-breathing frogs visit?"

Students should then use their ideas from the organizer to write a first-person narrative of a visit from Douglas from the perspective of one of the play's characters. To scaffold this activity further, you might provide students with a model of how a Cinderella "After-the-End" story might begin:

> *They say the story of Cinderella ended happily ever after, but some of us were not at all happy. The story you are about to hear is a story of a misrepresented sister, the loving, but forgotten step-sister. Let me put my feet up (yes, they're still recovering from being forced into glass shoes two sizes too small) and tell you how Cinderella has made a royal mess of marriage.*

Jon Scieszka's *The Frog Prince Continued* (Scholastic, 1991) makes a terrific full-length example of an extended fractured fairy tale.

**Extend it!** Ask students to write about the same events happening but from two different character points of view. For example, students may write a one-page story from the point of view of Douglas and then a one-page story about the same events from the point of view of Mr. Roberts. An extension to this activity is to ask students to choose a character from the play and rewrite the events from the perspective of that character in story form (as in Scieszka's *The True Story of the Three Little Pigs* (Scholastic, 1989).

Name_____     Date_____

# What Happens After "Happily Ever After"?

Ever wonder what happened to Cinderella's step sisters after she married the prince? What about Rumpelstiltskin or Jack? There's always another story just waiting to be discovered after the end of any fairy tale—and it's up to your imagination to create it!

**Here's how to get started:** Pick your favorite fairy tale and summarize the ending. Then choose a character or characters to focus on (for example, you might choose Cinderella again or the defeated, but still-jealous step sisters). Pick a new problem and find ways that the characters try to solve it. Then pick a final solution.

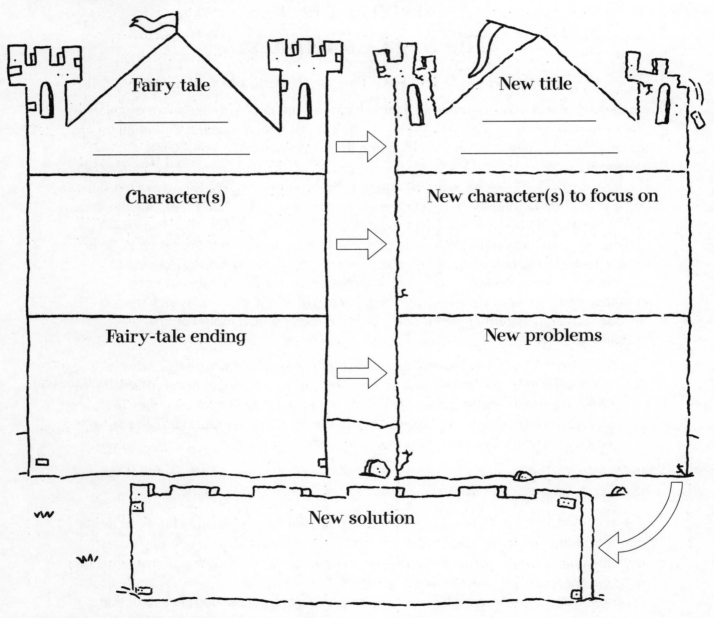

Fairy tale

_____

Character(s)

Fairy-tale ending

New title

_____

New character(s) to focus on

New problems

New solution

**Now that you've planned the story, write it!**

**Challenge!** Try to write from the point of view of one of the characters involved in the new story. Assume that character's identity and write it like you experienced it yourself.

# Resources!

## ☙ I. More Quick Costume Ideas ❧

Browse through the tips that follow to find quick and easy ideas for costumes if you wish to go beyond simple street clothes.

## Animal Characters

**Ears I:** Use thick construction paper, tagboard, or felt cut in the shape of ears. Bend a pipe cleaner stem to match the cut-out ear. Spread glue around the edge of the ear and attach it to the pipe-cleaner stem. Fasten each ear by twisting the pipe cleaner ends around the band.

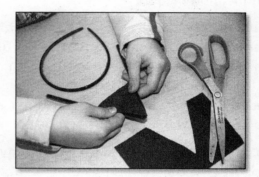

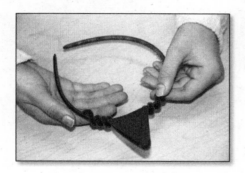

**Ears II:** Lightly inflated balloons (or balloons filled with rice) make great ears that hang down and flop. Attach to the head with barrettes or tape to a headband.

**Fur coat:** Wear dark-colored sweatshirts and matching pants. The same kinds of animals in a play wear the same colored sweatshirts (for example, the three pigs might wear sweatshirts that are pink, brown, or stained-all-over).

**Noses and whiskers:** Use an eyebrow pencil to draw whiskers and darken in the tip of a nose on students. (Be careful the pencil has not been used previously and never use one around the eye area.)

**Tails:** Can be attached with safety pins or heavy tape to waistbands or belts. Tails can be made of lightly inflated balloons, socks, construction paper, tinfoil (that may or may not be painted), ties, or braided yarn.

**Spots and coloring:** Animal spots and colored markings can be made out of construction paper, pieces of felt, or light pieces of fabric and taped on with masking tape or duct tape. A light sprinkling of baby powder can change dark hair into lighter hair. Nylons, when cut and put over the hair and ears can give the illusion of "baldness" for characters that have little hair (such as pigs).

## Human Characters

**Children:** May carry large-size lollipops (made out of large cardboard circles colored and glued to plain stir sticks or tongue depressors), and have freckles marked with eyebrow pencil.

**Official characters:** Reporters, police officers, and so forth, may wear adult-size blazers or ties, with identification badges.

**Goofy characters:** May carry funny purses or pouches or wear brightly colored ties or bathrobes. They may also wear sunglasses or eyeglasses, with or without the lenses. Long gloves and construction-paper headband crowns decorated with glitter and curling ribbon work well for queens and princesses.

**Butlers, maids, househelpers:** May carry trays (easily made by covering round pieces of cardboard with tinfoil) and wear white gloves and dark uniforms.

## Freebie Character Ideas

**(Things to try that cost absolutely nothing!)**

**Accents:** Students can add distinctive voice inflections or accents to character lines.

**Walks**: Students may walk on their tip toes, swagger, or walk with their noses in the air to appear "snooty" or they can develop another form of walk that accentuates the personality of their character.

**Funny Sounds:** Students may add loud sighs, sneezes, gulps, snickers, growls, or other noises at appropriate places.

**Gestures:** Students may create a distinctive position for their hands or arms to add to their characters. For example, one character may keep his or her arms crossed, or keep one arm and hand up. Another character might have a unique facial expression or grimace. Students can pretend to chew and smack gum or stick out their tongues in appropriate places.

# ∾ II. More Simple Set Ideas ∾

Whether you are looking for simple or elaborate play sets, you can gather ideas for both from the lists below. If you need help, consider hosting a set night or afternoon when parents and kids work on the set.

## Sets You Can Make with Things Found at School

Blackboards on wheels easily convert into walls for houses or storefronts by covering them with bulletin board paper that has been decorated appropriately. These can do double duty as each side can be decorated in a different way and serve as two different walls.

Paper boxes (or any kind of box) become a house wall when covered with paper or painted and stacked.

Beds can be as simple as a blanket or piece of bulletin board paper laid on the floor.

## Slightly More Ambitious Sets

Many store owners are willing to provide appliance boxes that can be disassembled and used as large pieces of "wood" for houses, castles, and so forth. Simply rip the seams and use the box like a large piece of plywood. If you are feeling particularly handy, you can even nail cardboard to small 2' x 4's and create a three-dimensional structure. Cardboard can also be painted and decorated and then taped to an overturned chair or desk for support.

## Sound Effects

Students may experiment with different objects to see what kinds of sounds they make. Experiment with plastic bags, crinkling paper, tinfoil, footsteps, rice and so forth. You may to even collect these sounds on a class audiotape. Encourage students to listen outside for any interesting sounds they can hear and then audiotape them. Public libraries often have an excellent selection of tapes and CD's that have sound effects and background music.

## Props

Many of the plays in this book have opportunities for living props and scenery for students who prefer not to have speaking

parts. Some examples of living props include: trees, bushes, rocks, clocks (the grandfather kind), gingerbread cookies, and street signs. If students are able to do it without giggling, they may also act as doors, coat racks, and furniture.

# Bibliography

## ∾ Traditional Fairy Tales ∾

Traditional fairy tales have been published in a variety of forms. Below you will find just a few examples.

Augenstine, Erin. *Snow White*. Kansas City: Ariel Books, 1991.

Brett, Jan. *Beauty and the Beast*. New York: Clarion Books, 1989.

_____. *Goldilocks and the Three Bears*. New York: G.P. Putnam's Sons, 1987.

Ehrlich, Amy. *Rapunzel*. New York: Dial Books for Young Readers,1989.

Kirstein, Lincoln. (Charles Perrault). *Puss in Boots*. Boston: Little Brown and Company, 1992.

Perrault, Charles. *Cinderella*. New York: Dial Books for Young Readers, 1985.

Sanderson, Ruth. *The Twelve Dancing Princesses*. Canada: Little Brown and Company, 1990.

Zelinsky, Paul. *Rumpelstiltskin*. New York: Dutton Children's Books,1986.

## ∾ Nontraditional Fairy Tales ∾

The books that follow are twists and humorous retellings of traditional fairy tales.

Minters, Frances. *Sleepless Beauty*. New York: Viking-Penguin Group, 1996.

Scieszka, Jon. *The Frog Prince Continued*. New York: Scholastic, 1991.

_____. *The True Story of the Three Little Pigs*. New York: Scholastic, 1989.

Stanley, Diane. *Rumpelstiltskin's Daughter*. New York: William Morrow, 1997.

Thaler, Mike. *Schmoe White and the Seven Dorfs*. New York: Scholastic, 1997.

Yolen, Jane. *Sleeping Ugly*. New York: G.P. Putnam's Sons, 1981.

Jackson, Ellen. *Cinder Edna*. New York: William Morrow, 1994.

### Cinderella Tales and Variations

There are more than 500 versions of the Cinderella tale. Here are just a few.

Climo, Shirley. *The Egyptian Cinderella*. New York: HarperCollins Children's Books, 1989.
  (Egyptian: This is reportedly the first-known version of Cinderella.)

_____. *The Irish Cinderlad*. New York: HarperCollins Publishers. 1996. (Irish)

Coburn, Jewell Reinhart. *Angkat, The Cambodian Cinderella*. California: Shen's Books. 1998.
  (Cambodian)

Hickox, Rebecca. *The Golden Sandal, A Middle Eastern Cinderella Story*. New York: Holiday House, 1998. (Middle Eastern)

Huck, Charlotte. *Princess Furball*. New York: Greenwillow Books, 1989. (Russian)

Marctin, Rafe. *The Rough-Face Girl*. New York: G.P. Putnam's Sons, 1992. (Native American)

San Souci, Robert D. *The Talking Eggs*. New York: Dial Books for Young Readers, 1989. (American—Southern)

_____. *Cendrillan*. New York: Simon & Schuster Books for Young Readers, 1998. (Caribbean)

Steptoe, John. *Mufaro's Beautiful Daughters*. New York: Scholastic, 1987. (African)

## Multicultural Fairy Tales

Included below are several excellent fairy tales from various cultures.

Hamilton, Virginia. *The Girl Who Spun Gold*. New York: Blue Sky Press, 2000.

Heyer, Marcilee. *The Girl, The Fish, and the Crown: A Spanish Folktale*. New York: Puffin Books, 1995.

Yep, Laurence. *The Dragon Prince: A Chinese Beauty and the Beast Tale*. New York: HarperCollins Publishers, 1997.

Young, Ed. *Lon Po Po: A Red-Riding Hood Story From China*. New York: Philomel Books, 1989.

## Fairy Tale Theory/Collection Books

These resources offer adults a historical understanding of fairy tales.

Bosma, Bette. *Fairy Tales, Fables, Legends, and Myths: Using Folk Literature in Your Classroom*. New York: Teachers College Press, 1992.

Dockray, Tracy Arah. *Grimm's Grimmest*. San Francisco: Chronicle Books, 1997.

Tatar, Marcia. *The Hard Facts of the Grimms' Fairy Tales*. New Jersey: Princeton University Press, 1987.

Zipes, Jack. *When Dreams Came True: Classical Fairy Tales and Their Tradition*. New York: Routledge, 1999.

# Notes